Solo Air Fryer Cookbook: Portioned Recipes for One

Quick & Easy, Single-Serve Meals with Original Images

by **Miguel Dobos**

Copyright © by Miguel Dobos

All rights reserved. No part of this publication may be reproduced, distributed, or transmitted in any form or by any means, including photocopying, recording, or other electronic or mechanical methods, without the prior written permission of the publisher, except in the case of brief quotations embodied in critical reviews and specific other noncommercial uses permitted by copyright law.

This book is available in Kindle and Paperback formats and must not be resold or given to others without the author's consent. If you would like to share this book with another person, please purchase an additional copy for each recipient. If you're reading this book and have not purchased it, or it was not purchased for your use only, please return it to your preferred book retailer and purchase your copy. Thank you for respecting the hard work of this author.

The information in this book is provided as is, and the publisher and author disclaim all warranties, express or implied, including any implied warranties of fitness for a particular purpose. Neither the publisher nor the author shall be liable for any loss of profit or other commercial damages, including but not limited to special, incidental, consequential, or other damages.

As per Amazon KDP rules and regulations, the images and content within this book are the author's property and were created, compiled, or provided by Miguel Dobos with the right of publication and distribution. The recipes and content within this book are intended for personal use and not for commercial replication or use.

Introduction

Welcome to the "Solo Air Fryer Cookbook: Perfectly Portioned Recipes for One," your ultimate guide to mastering quick and easy single-serve meals using your air fryer. Whether you're cooking for yourself due to a busy schedule, personal preference, or simply because you're enjoying the single life, this cookbook is designed to cater to your needs, offering a variety of dishes that suit any taste and occasion.

In this cookbook, Miguel Dobos shares a collection of his favorite air fryer recipes that are simple to prepare and incredibly delicious. From hearty breakfasts to get your day started right to nutritious lunches, indulgent dinners, and even decadent desserts, each recipe is perfectly portioned to serve one, ensuring you enjoy a full-flavored meal without worrying about excessive leftovers.

The air fryer is an extraordinary tool that allows you to cook faster while achieving the crispy and tasty results of deep frying without the unhealthy oils. This book harnesses the power of this popular appliance to provide you with quick, easy, healthy, and satisfying meals.

"Quick & Easy, Single-Serve Meals with Original Images" guides you through the cooking process but also includes original images that offer a visual reference for each dish. These images inspire and assist you in creating meals that look as good as they taste.

Each recipe in this collection has been carefully tested and includes step-by-step instructions that make cooking enjoyable and hassle-free. Whether new to air frying or looking to expand your single-serving repertoire, this book will provide the inspiration and information you need to cook delicious meals efficiently.

Join Miguel Dobos on this culinary journey and discover how to make the most of your air fryer with recipes that promise to keep your meals exciting and your kitchen adventures fun!

Table of Contents

Introduction 3

Chapter 01: Air Fryer Breakfast 8

    Egg Muffins with Spinach and Bacon 8

    French Toast Sticks with Syrup and Fruit 10

    Puff Pastry Pies Filled with Caramelized Apples 12

    Grilled Corn Summer Pasta Salad 14

    Avocado OMELETTE with Tomatoes 16

    Blueberry Scones with Lemon Glaze 18

    Egg and Crispy Potato Burrito Filled with Rice 20

    Pecan Schnecken Sticky Buns 22

    Stuffed Baked Potatoes Garnish 24

    Fried Bread with Minced Pork 26

Chapter 02: Mediterranean Lunch Recipes 28

    Grilled Dumplings Pork and Vegetables 28

    Bruschetta Chicken Breast with Tomatoes 30

    Sesame Asian Salad with Chicken Carrot 32

    Portobello Mushroom Black Bean Burger 34

    Loaded Sweet Potato Skins Stuffed 36

    Sausage Onions and Peppers Hoagie Sandwich 38

    Samosa Filled with Chicken and Vegetables 40

    Grilled Cheese and Tomato Sandwich 42

    Asian Minced Meat Lettuce Wrap 44

    Spicy Chicken Wings with BBQ Sauce 46

Chapter 03: Air Fryer Dinner Recipes 48

    Breaded German Wiener Schnitzel with Potatoes 48

    Crispy Salt and Pepper Tofu 50

    Spaghetti Full Shrimp with Sundried Tomatoes 52

    Roasted Lamb Ribs with Spices and Greens 54

    Roasted Cornish Hen with Apples 56

Roasted Pork with Potatoes 58

Stuffed Bell Peppers with Quinoa Tomatoes 60

Fried Cod Fillet with Asparagus and Tomatoes 62

Beef and Broccoli Stir Fry 64

Chicken and Bell Peppers in Skewers 66

Chapter 04: Air Fryer Snacks Recipes 68

Fried Zucchini Sticks Chips 68

Sweet Potato Tater Tots with Ketchup 70

Delicious Jalapeno Poppers 72

Baked Mushrooms Stuffed 74

Coconut Shrimp with Dipping Sauces 76

Bacon Wrapped Dates with Goat Cheese 78

Buffalo Cauliflower Wings 80

Dried Apple Chips with Cinnamon 82

Fried Crispy Onion Rings with Ketchup 84

Turkish Fried Borek Rolls with Meat Filling 86

Chapter 05: Air Fryer Appetizers Recipes 88

Grilled Violet Asparagus Wrapped with Bacon 88

Chicken Spinach Artichoke Creamy Soup 90

Seafood Mini Crab Cake Balls 92

Barbecue Chicken Flatbreads with Red Onion 94

Spicy Korean Chicken Drumsticks 96

Chicken Mushroom Stuffed Peppers 98

Mozzarella Breaded Sticks 100

Crispy Garlic Bacon Bread 102

Roasted Fig Halves with Drizzle Honey 104

Stir-fried Beef with Vegetables 106

Conclusion 108

How to Cook in an Air Fryer?

Cooking with an air fryer is simple and efficient, making it a popular choice for quick and healthier meals. Here's a general guide on how to cook in an air fryer:

Preparation

- **Preheat the Air Fryer:** Most recipes benefit from preheating, as it ensures the cooking chamber is at the right temperature before you add your food. This step usually takes about 3 to 5 minutes, depending on the model.
- **Prepare Your Ingredients:** Depending on your cooking, this might involve marinating, seasoning, or coating your ingredients in oil and breadcrumbs or flour for crispiness. Ensure food is dry to help achieve a golden, crispy texture.

Loading the Air Fryer

- **Avoid Overcrowding:** To cook food evenly, place it in a single layer in the basket. Overcrowding can lead to uneven cooking and less crispiness.
- **Use a Little Oil:** While air fryers require less oil than traditional frying, a light spritz can help achieve a more golden, crispy exterior. Use an oil sprayer or brush to coat the food lightly.

Cooking

- **Set Time and Temperature:** Follow recipe-specific temperature and cooking time recommendations. If you're experimenting, a good rule of thumb is to start at a lower temperature and adjust as needed.
- **Shake or Turn:** Shake the basket or turn the items with tongs periodically throughout cooking for evenly cooked results. This is especially important for smaller items like fries or vegetables that can stick together.

Checking Doneness

- **Test for Doneness:** Cooking times can vary based on the food type, quantity, and individual air fryer model. Check your food towards the end of cooking and adjust the time as needed.
- **Use a Thermometer:** Ensure food safety by checking internal temperatures with a food thermometer for meats.

Post-Cooking

- **Let it Rest:** Some foods, like meat, might benefit from sitting a few minutes after cooking to redistribute juices.
- **Serving:** Serve immediately. Air-fried foods are best enjoyed crispy right out of the machine.

Cleaning

- **Clean Regularly:** Ensure you clean the air fryer after each use to prevent build-up and maintain performance. Most baskets and trays are dishwasher safe.

Recipes and Ideas

Experiment with different recipes. Air fryers are great for making appetizers like chicken wings, main courses such as salmon or pork chops, and even desserts like quick cakes or roasted fruit. Their versatility allows them to bake, roast, and grill, extending their use beyond frying.

By following these steps, you'll be able to make the most out of your air fryer, creating delicious, healthy meals with ease.

Chapter 01: Air Fryer Breakfast

Egg Muffins with Spinach and Bacon

Start your morning with these delicious and nutritious egg muffins packed with fresh spinach and crispy bacon. They're a perfect grab-and-go breakfast!

Servings: 1

Prepping Time: 10 minutes

Cook Time: 15 minutes

Difficulty: Easy

Ingredients:

- 2 large eggs
- 1/4 cup chopped fresh spinach
- 2 slices of bacon, cooked and crumbled
- 2 tbsp shredded cheddar cheese
- Salt and pepper to taste

Step-by-Step Preparation:

1. Preheat your air fryer to 360°F (182°C).
2. In a bowl, whisk the eggs with salt and pepper.
3. Stir in the chopped spinach, crumbled bacon, and shredded cheese.
4. Pour the mixture into a greased muffin tin suitable for air fryers.
5. Place the tin in the air fryer and cook for 15 minutes or until the eggs are set.
6. Carefully remove the muffin tin from the air fryer and let it cool for a minute before serving.

Nutritional Facts: (Per serving)

- Calories: 320
- Protein: 22g
- Carbohydrates: 2g
- Fat: 24g
- Cholesterol: 372mg
- Sodium: 560mg

Enjoy these tasty egg muffins as a quick breakfast or a healthy snack. They're easy to make and packed with protein, making them an excellent start to your day!

French Toast Sticks with Syrup and Fruit

Indulge in a delightful breakfast of French toast sticks, served with a syrup drizzle and fresh fruit. This sweet, satisfying meal will turn your morning into a special occasion!

Servings: 1

Prepping Time: 5 minutes

Cook Time: 8 minutes

Difficulty: Easy

Ingredients:

- 2 slices of thick-cut bread, cut into strips
- 1 egg
- 1/4 cup milk
- 1/2 tsp vanilla extract
- 1/2 tsp cinnamon
- 1 tbsp maple syrup

- 1/2 cup mixed fresh berries

Step-by-Step Preparation:

1. Whisk together the egg, milk, vanilla extract, and cinnamon in a shallow dish.
2. Dip bread strips into the egg mixture, coating them well.
3. Place the coated bread strips in the air fryer basket in a single layer.
4. Air fry at 360°F (182°C) for 8 minutes, turning halfway through until golden and crispy.
5. Serve the French toast sticks hot with maple syrup and a side of fresh berries.

Nutritional Facts: (Per serving)

- Calories: 280
- Protein: 8g
- Carbohydrates: 45g
- Fat: 8g
- Fiber: 3g
- Sugar: 18g

This quick and easy French toast breakfast is perfect for mornings when you want something extra but don't have much time. Enjoy the golden, crispy texture and the burst of flavors from the syrup and fresh fruit!

Puff Pastry Pies Filled with Caramelized Apples

Experience a delightful twist on breakfast with puff pastry pies filled with caramelized apples. This recipe brings a touch of elegance and sweetness to your morning routine!

Servings: 1

Prepping Time: 10 minutes

Cook Time: 15 minutes

Difficulty: Easy

Ingredients:

- 1 large puff pastry sheet, cut into two squares
- 1 apple, peeled and sliced
- 1 tbsp butter
- 2 tbsp brown sugar
- 1/2 tsp cinnamon

- 1 pinch of nutmeg
- 1 egg, beaten (for egg wash)

Step-by-Step Preparation:

1. Melt butter in a pan over medium heat. Add apple slices, brown sugar, cinnamon, and nutmeg. Cook until the apples are tender and caramelized, about 5 minutes. Set aside to cool.
2. Place half of the caramelized apples in the square of one puff pastry.
3. Fold the pastry over the apples to form a pie, sealing the edges with a fork.
4. Brush the top with the beaten egg for a golden finish.
5. Air fry at 360°F (182°C) for 15 minutes or until the pastry is puffed and golden brown.
6. Let cool slightly before serving.

Nutritional Facts: (Per serving)

- Calories: 510
- Protein: 7g
- Carbohydrates: 58g
- Fat: 28g
- Fiber: 3g
- Sugar: 24g

Start your day with these scrumptious puff pastry pies, a sweet and satisfying dish that combines the comfort of baked apples with the crispiness of puff pastry. Perfect for a leisurely morning or a decadent brunch!

Grilled Corn Summer Pasta Salad

Savor the flavors of summer with this vibrant Grilled Corn Summer Pasta Salad. It's a refreshing and filling breakfast that combines the smoky taste of grilled corn with fresh vegetables and pasta, all dressed in a light vinaigrette.

Servings: 1

Prepping Time: 10 minutes

Cook Time: 15 minutes

Difficulty: Easy

Ingredients:

- 1/2 cup cooked penne pasta
- 1 ear of corn, husked
- 1/4 cup cherry tomatoes, halved
- 1/4 cup cucumber, diced
- 2 tbsp red onion, finely chopped
- 1 tbsp olive oil

- 1 tbsp white vinegar
- Salt and pepper to taste
- Fresh basil leaves, chopped (for garnish)

Step-by-Step Preparation:

1. Brush the corn with olive oil and season with salt and pepper.
2. Place the corn in the air fryer and cook at 400°F (204°C) for 10 minutes, turning halfway, until charred and tender.
3. Once cool, slice the kernels off the cob.
4. Combine the grilled corn kernels, cooked pasta, cherry tomatoes, cucumber, and red onion in a bowl.
5. Whisk together olive oil, vinegar, salt, and pepper in a small bowl to create the dressing.
6. Pour the dressing over the pasta salad and toss well to coat.
7. Garnish with fresh basil before serving.

Nutritional Facts: (Per serving)

- Calories: 325
- Protein: 6g
- Carbohydrates: 45g
- Fat: 14g
- Fiber: 4g
- Sugar: 8g

This Grilled Corn Summer Pasta Salad is the perfect way to kickstart your day with a hearty and refreshing meal. It's ideal for those mornings when you want something light yet satisfying. Enjoy the burst of fresh flavors with every bite!

Avocado OMELETTE with Tomatoes

Whip up this delicious Avocado OMELETTE, combining creamy avocado, tangy blue cheese, sweet tomatoes, and fresh green peas for a nutritious and gourmet start to your day. It's a colorful and flavorful breakfast option that's easy to prepare!

>**Servings:** 1
>
>**Prepping Time:** 5 minutes
>
>**Cook Time:** 8 minutes
>
>**Difficulty:** Easy

Ingredients:

- 2 large eggs
- 1/2 avocado, diced
- 1/4 cup cherry tomatoes, halved
- 2 tbsp crumbled blue cheese
- 1/4 cup green peas, fresh or thawed
- Salt and pepper to taste

- 1 tbsp olive oil (for cooking)

Step-by-Step Preparation:

1. In a bowl, beat the eggs with salt and pepper.
2. Heat the olive oil in a small, air fryer-safe pan over medium heat.
3. Pour the eggs into the pan, then scatter the diced avocado, cherry tomatoes, green peas, and crumbled blue cheese evenly over the top.
4. Place the pan in the air fryer and cook at 360°F (182°C) for about 8 minutes or until the eggs are fully set.
5. Carefully remove the pan from the air fryer, let the OMELETTE cool slightly, then gently slide it onto a plate.

Nutritional Facts: (Per serving)

- Calories: 400
- Protein: 18g
- Carbohydrates: 12g
- Fat: 32g
- Fiber: 6g
- Sugar: 4g

Enjoy this Avocado OMELETTE as a luxurious yet simple breakfast. The combination of fresh veggies and rich blue cheese provides a fantastic fusion of flavors to satisfy your morning appetite. Perfect for a healthy and fulfilling start to your day!

Blueberry Scones with Lemon Glaze

Indulge in a delightful treat of Blueberry Scones topped with a zesty lemon glaze. These scones are perfect for a leisurely breakfast or a mid-morning snack, combining sweet blueberries with lemon's fresh, tangy taste.

Servings: 1

Prepping Time: 10 minutes

Cook Time: 15 minutes

Difficulty: Easy

Ingredients:

- 1 cup all-purpose flour
- 1/4 cup granulated sugar
- 1 tsp baking powder
- 1/4 tsp salt
- 1/4 cup cold unsalted butter, cubed
- 1/3 cup fresh blueberries

- 1/4 cup heavy cream, plus extra for brushing
- 1/2 tsp vanilla extract
- 1/2 tsp grated lemon zest

For the Lemon Glaze:

- 1/4 cup powdered sugar
- 1 tbsp lemon juice

Step-by-Step Preparation:

1. Combine flour, sugar, baking powder, and salt in a mixing bowl.
2. Cut in the butter until the mixture resembles coarse crumbs.
3. Gently fold in blueberries, cream, vanilla, and lemon zest until the dough comes together.
4. Form the dough into a round scone shape and place it on a greased air fryer basket.
5. Brush the top of the scone with a little extra cream.
6. Air fry at 360°F (182°C) for about 15 minutes or until golden brown.
7. Mix powdered sugar and lemon juice to create the glaze.
8. Drizzle the glaze over the warm scone before serving.

Nutritional Facts: (Per serving)

- Calories: 605
- Protein: 8g
- Carbohydrates: 85g
- Fat: 26g
- Fiber: 2g
- Sugar: 37g

Treat yourself to this exquisite combination of sweet blueberries and refreshing lemon. These Blueberry Scones with Lemon Glaze are a splendid way to start any day, offering flavor and sweetness.

Egg and Crispy Potato Burrito Filled with Rice

Kick off your morning with this hearty and satisfying Egg and Crispy Potato Burrito with rice. It's a filling breakfast that packs a flavorful punch, ideal for fueling a busy day ahead!

Servings: 1

Prepping Time: 10 minutes

Cook Time: 20 minutes

Difficulty: Easy

Ingredients:

- 1 large tortilla
- 1 egg, beaten
- 1/2 cup diced potatoes
- 1/4 cup cooked rice
- 1/4 cup shredded cheddar cheese
- 2 tbsp salsa

- Salt and pepper to taste
- 1 tbsp olive oil

Step-by-Step Preparation:

1. Toss the diced potatoes with olive oil, salt, and pepper. Air fry at 400°F (204°C) for 10 minutes or until crispy.
2. Remove the potatoes and set aside.
3. Pour the beaten egg into a small, greased air fryer-safe dish and cook at 370°F (188°C) for 3 minutes or until set.
4. Warm the tortilla in the air fryer for 1 minute to make it pliable.
5. Layer the cooked egg, crispy potatoes, rice, shredded cheese, and salsa on the tortilla.
6. Roll the tortilla tightly to form a burrito.
7. Place the burrito back in the air fryer and cook at 360°F (182°C) for 5 minutes until the outside is slightly crispy and golden.
8. Serve hot.

Nutritional Facts: (Per serving)

- Calories: 520
- Protein: 18g
- Carbohydrates: 58g
- Fat: 24g
- Fiber: 4g
- Sugar: 3g

Enjoy this delicious Egg and Crispy Potato Burrito as a robust start to your morning or a fulfilling brunch option. The combination of fluffy eggs, crispy potatoes, and warm rice wrapped in a soft tortilla will satisfy you until your next meal!

Pecan Schnecken Sticky Buns

Indulge in the sweet aroma and delightful taste of Pecan Schnecken Sticky Buns. This recipe offers a luxurious twist on the classic sticky bun, featuring rich pecans and a decadent caramel glaze. It's the perfect treat to enjoy with your morning coffee!

Servings: 1

Prepping Time: 15 minutes

Cook Time: 20 minutes

Difficulty: Easy

Ingredients:

- 1 small batch of dough (enough to make 1 large bun)
- 1 tbsp butter, softened
- 2 tbsp brown sugar
- 1/4 tsp cinnamon
- 2 tbsp chopped pecans
- 1 tbsp heavy cream

Step-by-Step Preparation:

1. Roll out the dough into a small rectangle on a lightly floured surface.
2. Spread the softened butter over the dough.
3. Mix the brown sugar and cinnamon and sprinkle evenly over the buttered dough.
4. Sprinkle chopped pecans over the sugar mixture.
5. Roll the dough tightly from one end to the other and slice it into one large piece.
6. Place the bun in a small, greased air fryer-safe dish.
7. Drizzle heavy cream over the top of the bun.
8. Air fry at 350°F (177°C) for 20 minutes or until golden brown and the sugar has caramelized.
9. Allow to cool slightly before serving.

Nutritional Facts: (Per serving)

- Calories: 465
- Protein: 5g
- Carbohydrates: 58g
- Fat: 25g
- Fiber: 2g
- Sugar: 29g

Savor each bite of these Pecan Schnecken Sticky Buns as they melt in your mouth with gooey, caramelized goodness. Whether it's a leisurely Sunday morning or a special breakfast, these sticky buns make the moment decadent.

Stuffed Baked Potatoes Garnish

Transform your morning with this hearty Stuffed Baked Potatoes Garnish. This exquisite breakfast combines fluffy potatoes with a rich filling of your favorite toppings. It's a comforting and versatile dish that is perfect for a fulfilling start to the day.

Servings: 1

Prepping Time: 10 minutes

Cook Time: 40 minutes

Difficulty: Easy

Ingredients:

- 1 large russet potato
- 1 tbsp olive oil
- Salt and pepper to taste
- 2 tbsp sour cream
- 1/4 cup shredded cheddar cheese
- 2 tbsp chopped green onions

- 2 slices cooked bacon, crumbled
- 1 tbsp butter

Step-by-Step Preparation:

1. Wash and dry the potato, then prick several times with a fork.
2. Rub the potato with olive oil and season with salt and pepper.
3. Place the potato in the air fryer and cook at 400°F (204°C) for 40 minutes or until tender.
4. Once cooked, slice the top of the potato and scoop out some of the insides, leaving a small rim to support the structure.
5. Mix the scooped potato with sour cream, butter, half the cheese, and half the green onions.
6. Spoon the mixture back into the potato shell.
7. Top with remaining cheese and bacon crumbles.
8. Return to the air fryer for 5 minutes or until the cheese is melted.
9. Garnish with the remaining green onions before serving.

Nutritional Facts: (Per serving)

- Calories: 485
- Protein: 15g
- Carbohydrates: 38g
- Fat: 31g
- Fiber: 3g
- Sugar: 2g

Enjoy this Stuffed Baked Potato as a luxurious breakfast or brunch centerpiece. Its creamy, cheesy filling and crispy skin delight every bite, ensuring a satisfying and delicious start to any day.

Fried Bread with Minced Pork

Dive into the savory world of Fried Bread with Minced Pork, a delightful fusion of crispy bread and flavorful pork that will revolutionize your breakfast. It's an easy, satisfying meal that packs a delicious punch to start your day right!

Servings: 1

Prepping Time: 15 minutes

Cook Time: 10 minutes

Difficulty: Easy

Ingredients:

- 1 slice of thick bread
- 100g minced pork
- 1 tbsp soy sauce
- 1 tsp minced garlic
- 1 tbsp chopped green onions
- 1 tbsp vegetable oil

- Salt and pepper to taste

Step-by-Step Preparation:

1. Heat the vegetable oil in a pan over medium heat.
2. Add minced garlic and pork to the pan. Season with soy sauce, salt, and pepper.
3. Cook the pork until it's browned and fully cooked, stirring frequently, about 5-7 minutes.
4. While the pork cooks, place the bread slice in the air fryer and cook at 180°C (356°F) for 3 minutes, until crisp.
5. Top the crispy bread with minced pork Once the bread is fried and the pork is cooked.
6. Garnish with chopped green onions.

Nutritional Facts: (Per serving)

- Calories: 450
- Protein: 22g
- Carbohydrates: 35g
- Fat: 25g
- Fiber: 2g
- Sugar: 3g

Savor the delightful crunch of fried bread topped with juicy, savory minced pork for a breakfast that is both fulfilling and delicious. This dish not only satisfies your morning hunger but also leaves you energized for the day ahead.

Chapter 02: Mediterranean Lunch Recipes

Grilled Dumplings Pork and Vegetables

Enjoy a savory treat with these Grilled Dumplings filled with pork and vegetables, a delightful blend of flavors and textures. These dumplings make for a satisfying and tasty lunch, providing the perfect bite-sized enjoyment cooked right in your air fryer!

Servings: 1

Prepping Time: 20 minutes

Cook Time: 10 minutes

Difficulty: Easy

Ingredients:

- 6 dumpling wrappers
- 1/4 cup ground pork

- 1/4 cup shredded cabbage
- 2 tbsp finely chopped carrots
- 1 green onion, finely chopped
- 1 tsp soy sauce
- 1/2 tsp sesame oil
- 1/2 tsp minced ginger
- Salt and pepper to taste

Step-by-Step Preparation:

1. Combine the ground pork, shredded cabbage, carrots, green onion, soy sauce, sesame oil, ginger, salt, and pepper in a mixing bowl.
2. Place a small spoonful of the filling in the center of each dumpling wrapper.
3. Wet the edges of the wrapper with water and fold over to seal, pressing out any air.
4. Preheat the air fryer to 370°F (188°C).
5. Arrange the dumplings in a single layer in the air fryer basket and cook for 10 minutes, flipping halfway through, until golden and crispy.
6. Serve hot with a side of soy sauce for dipping.

Nutritional Facts: (Per serving)

- Calories: 320
- Protein: 16g
- Carbohydrates: 34g
- Fat: 12g
- Fiber: 2g
- Sugar: 2g

These Grilled Dumplings are perfect for a quick, flavorful lunch that's sure to please. Easy to make and even easier to enjoy, they bring a touch of gourmet to your daily dining experience!

Bruschetta Chicken Breast with Tomatoes

Elevate your lunch with this Bruschetta Chicken Breast. It combines juicy tomatoes and a balsamic glaze for a fresh, Italian-inspired dish. This recipe is perfect for a quick yet flavorful meal that will impress!

Servings: 1

Prepping Time: 10 minutes

Cook Time: 12 minutes

Difficulty: Easy

Ingredients:

- 1 boneless, skinless chicken breast
- 1/2 cup diced ripe tomatoes
- 1 tbsp chopped fresh basil
- 1 garlic clove, minced
- 2 tbsp balsamic vinegar
- 1 tbsp olive oil

- Salt and pepper to taste

Step-by-Step Preparation:

1. Preheat the air fryer to 360°F (182°C).
2. Season the chicken breast with salt and pepper.
3. Mix tomatoes, basil, garlic, 1 tablespoon balsamic vinegar, and 1 tablespoon olive oil in a small bowl.
4. Place the chicken in the air fryer and cook for 10 minutes.
5. Top the chicken with the tomato mixture and cook for 2 minutes.
6. Drizzle the remaining balsamic vinegar over the cooked chicken before serving.

Nutritional Facts: (Per serving)

- Calories: 295
- Protein: 26g
- Carbohydrates: 10g
- Fat: 16g
- Fiber: 2g
- Sugar: 7g

Savor this Bruschetta Chicken Breast as a delightful twist on classic flavors. It blends the tang of balsamic with the sweetness of tomatoes to create a perfectly balanced and nutritious meal. It's ideal for a delicious and healthy lunch that keeps you energized throughout the day!

Sesame Asian Salad with Chicken Carrot

Enjoy a light and refreshing Sesame Asian Salad, a vibrant mix of chicken, carrots, and cabbage, all tossed in a tangy sesame dressing. This salad is a perfect, quick, nutritious lunch option with flavor and crunch!

Servings: 1

Prepping Time: 10 minutes

Cook Time: 10 minutes

Difficulty: Easy

Ingredients:

- 1 small chicken breast
- 1/2 cup shredded carrots
- 1 cup shredded cabbage
- 1 tbsp sesame oil
- 2 tbsp soy sauce
- 1 tbsp rice vinegar

- 1 tsp honey
- 1 tbsp sesame seeds
- Salt and pepper to taste

Step-by-Step Preparation:

1. Season the chicken breast with salt and pepper.
2. Air fry the chicken at 360°F (182°C) for 10 minutes or until fully cooked. Let it cool, and then shred it.
3. Combine the shredded chicken, carrots, and cabbage in a large bowl.
4. Whisk together sesame oil, soy sauce, rice vinegar, and honey in a small bowl.
5. Pour the dressing over the salad and toss to coat evenly.
6. Sprinkle sesame seeds over the salad before serving.

Nutritional Facts: (Per serving)

- Calories: 320
- Protein: 28g
- Carbohydrates: 15g
- Fat: 16g
- Fiber: 3g
- Sugar: 7g

This Sesame Asian Salad is a delicious way to enjoy a healthy, light meal that keeps you satisfied without feeling heavy. Perfect for a quick lunch, it brings a delightful blend of flavors and textures to your table.

Portobello Mushroom Black Bean Burger

Dive into the rich flavors of this Portobello Mushroom Black Bean Burger, a vegetarian delight that packs a hearty punch. This burger is delicious and a healthy alternative to traditional meat burgers, perfect for a satisfying lunch!

Servings: 1

Prepping Time: 15 minutes

Cook Time: 8 minutes

Difficulty: Easy

Ingredients:

- 1 large Portobello mushroom cap, cleaned
- 1/2 cup canned black beans, drained and mashed
- 1 tbsp chopped red onion
- 1 clove garlic, minced
- 2 tbsp breadcrumbs
- 1 tbsp Worcestershire sauce (vegan if necessary)

- 1 tbsp olive oil
- Salt and pepper to taste
- 1 whole wheat burger bun

Step-by-Step Preparation:

1. Mix mashed black beans, red onion, garlic, breadcrumbs, Worcestershire sauce, salt, and pepper in a bowl.
2. Form the mixture into a patty to fit the size of the mushroom cap.
3. Brush the mushroom with olive oil and place it, gill side up, in the air fryer.
4. Place the bean patty on top of the mushroom.
5. Air fry at 360°F (182°C) for 8 minutes or until the patty is cooked and the mushroom is tender.
6. Serve the burger on a toasted whole wheat bun.

Nutritional Facts: (Per serving)

- Calories: 385
- Protein: 15g
- Carbohydrates: 58g
- Fat: 12g
- Fiber: 13g
- Sugar: 9g

Enjoy this Portobello Mushroom Black Bean Burger for a fulfilling and nutritious meal. It's a fantastic, easy-to-make lunch that combines the earthy mushroom flavors and the robustness of black beans, all packed in a delicious burger form. Perfect for any day of the week!

Loaded Sweet Potato Skins Stuffed

Savor the rich flavors in these Loaded Sweet Potato Skins stuffed with tender shredded chicken, smoked cheddar cheese, fresh cilantro, and red onion. This dish is a comforting, hearty lunch that will satisfy your cravings and fuel your afternoon!

Servings: 1

Prepping Time: 15 minutes

Cook Time: 20 minutes

Difficulty: Easy

Ingredients:

- 1 large sweet potato, halved
- 1/2 cup cooked shredded chicken fillet
- 1/4 cup smoked cheddar cheese, shredded
- 1 tbsp cilantro, chopped
- 2 tbsp red onion, finely chopped
- 1 tbsp olive oil

- Salt and pepper to taste
- 2 tbsp sour cream for topping

Step-by-Step Preparation:

1. Brush the sweet potato halves with olive oil and season with salt and pepper.
2. Place in the air fryer at 400°F (204°C) and cook for 15 minutes or until tender.
3. Scoop out the center of each half, leaving a small border to hold the fillings.
4. Mix the shredded chicken, smoked cheddar, cilantro, and red onion in a bowl.
5. Stuff this mixture back into the sweet potato skins.
6. Return to the air fryer for another 5 minutes until the cheese is melted and bubbly.
7. Top each skin with a tablespoon of sour cream before serving.

Nutritional Facts: (Per serving)

- Calories: 540
- Protein: 28g
- Carbohydrates: 49g
- Fat: 27g
- Fiber: 7g
- Sugar: 13g

These Loaded Sweet Potato Skins are a delightful way to enjoy a nutritious and indulgent lunch. The combination of sweet potato, creamy cheese, and savory chicken creates a perfect harmony of satisfying and delicious flavors!

Sausage Onions and Peppers Hoagie Sandwich

Dive into the classic flavors of a Sausage, Onions, and Peppers Hoagie Sandwich. This hearty sandwich combines savory sausage with sweet peppers and onions, all in a soft hoagie roll. It's the perfect quick and filling lunch to satisfy your midday hunger!

Servings: 1

Prepping Time: 10 minutes

Cook Time: 10 minutes

Difficulty: Easy

Ingredients:

- 1 Italian sausage link
- 1/4 cup sliced bell peppers (mix of colors)
- 1/4 cup sliced onions
- 1 hoagie roll
- 1 tbsp olive oil

- Salt and pepper to taste
- 1 tbsp mustard or mayonnaise (optional)

Step-by-Step Preparation:

1. Preheat the air fryer to 360°F (182°C).
2. Toss the sliced peppers and onions with olive oil, salt, and pepper.
3. Place the sausage, peppers, and onions in the air fryer basket.
4. Cook for 10 minutes, turning the sausage halfway through, until the vegetables are softened and the sausage is browned.
5. Slice the hoagie roll in half, and if desired, lightly toast it in the air fryer for 2 minutes.
6. Slice the sausage lengthwise and place it with the peppers and onions into the hoagie roll.
7. Add mustard or mayonnaise as preferred.

Nutritional Facts: (Per serving)

- Calories: 650
- Protein: 25g
- Carbohydrates: 46g
- Fat: 40g
- Fiber: 3g
- Sugar: 10g

Enjoy your Sausage, Onions, and Peppers Hoagie Sandwich as a robust and flavorful lunch. This sandwich packs a delightful crunch with every bite and brings a taste of classic street food right to your table. It's simple, delicious, and perfectly satisfying for any sandwich lover!

Samosa Filled with Chicken and Vegetables

Explore the delightful crunch and bold flavors of this Samosa Filled with Chicken and Vegetables, a lighter take on the traditional deep-fried favorite. This air fryer version offers a healthier alternative without compromising taste, making it an ideal savory lunch treat!

Servings: 1

Prepping Time: 20 minutes

Cook Time: 10 minutes

Difficulty: Easy

Ingredients:

- 1 samosa pastry sheet
- 1/4 cup cooked, shredded chicken
- 1/4 cup mixed vegetables (peas, carrots, corn)
- 1 tsp curry powder
- 1/4 tsp cumin
- 1/4 tsp coriander

- Salt and pepper to taste
- 1 tbsp oil (for brushing)

Step-by-Step Preparation:

1. Preheat the air fryer to 360°F (182°C).
2. Mix the shredded chicken, mixed vegetables, curry powder, cumin, coriander, salt, and pepper in a bowl.
3. Place the filling onto the center of the samosa pastry sheet.
4. Fold the pastry into a triangular shape, sealing the edges with water.
5. Brush the Samosa with oil to help it crisp up.
6. Air fry for 10 minutes, flipping halfway through, until golden and crispy.
7. Let cool slightly before serving.

Nutritional Facts: (Per serving)

- Calories: 290
- Protein: 15g
- Carbohydrates: 30g
- Fat: 12g
- Fiber: 3g
- Sugar: 2g

Enjoy this delicious Samosa Filled with Chicken and Vegetables, perfect for a quick and satisfying lunch. Packed with flavor and easy to prepare, it's a great way to treat yourself to something special in the middle of a busy day!

Grilled Cheese and Tomato Sandwich

Relish the comforting flavors of a Grilled Cheese and Tomato Sandwich, a classic combination that never fails to satisfy. Crisp, golden bread encases melting cheese and juicy tomato slices, creating a lunchtime masterpiece that's both simple and delicious.

Servings: 1

Prepping Time: 5 minutes

Cook Time: 8 minutes

Difficulty: Easy

Ingredients:

- 2 slices of whole-grain bread
- 2 slices of cheddar cheese
- 2 slices of ripe tomato
- 1 tbsp butter, softened

Step-by-Step Preparation:

1. Spread butter on one side of each bread slice.
2. Place one slice of bread, butter-side down, in the air fryer.
3. Layer the cheese and tomato slices on the bread.
4. Top with the second slice of bread, butter-side up.
5. Air fry at 360°F (182°C) for about 4 minutes on each side or until the bread is golden brown and the cheese has melted.
6. Remove from the air fryer and let sit for a minute before cutting.

Nutritional Facts: (Per serving)

- Calories: 400
- Protein: 16g
- Carbohydrates: 28g
- Fat: 26g
- Fiber: 4g
- Sugar: 5g

Enjoy this Grilled Cheese and Tomato Sandwich as a quick, easy, and comforting meal. Perfect for those days when you need a warm, satisfying lunch without much fuss. This timeless favorite will keep you coming back for more!

Asian Minced Meat Lettuce Wrap

Delight in the fresh and flavorful Asian Minced Meat Lettuce Wrap, an enticing lunch option that combines the crunch of lettuce with savory, seasoned meat. It's a light yet satisfying dish that brings a splash of Asian cuisine to your table with minimal effort.

Servings: 1

Prepping Time: 10 minutes

Cook Time: 10 minutes

Difficulty: Easy

Ingredients:

- 1/2 cup minced chicken or pork
- 1 tbsp soy sauce
- 1 tsp sesame oil
- 1 clove garlic, minced
- 1/2 tsp ginger, grated
- 1/4 cup diced water chestnuts

- 2 green onions, chopped
- 1 tbsp hoisin sauce
- 4-6 large lettuce leaves (like butter or iceberg)
- 1 tsp vegetable oil

Step-by-Step Preparation:

1. Mix the minced meat with soy sauce, sesame oil, garlic, and ginger in a small bowl.
2. Heat the vegetable oil in a pan and cook the meat mixture until browned about 5-7 minutes.
3. Add the water, chestnuts, and green onions to the pan, stir in hoisin sauce, and cook for another 2 minutes.
4. Spoon the cooked meat mixture into the lettuce leaves, folding them to form wraps.

Nutritional Facts: (Per serving)

- Calories: 310
- Protein: 23g
- Carbohydrates: 12g
- Fat: 18g
- Fiber: 3g
- Sugar: 5g

Savor these Asian Minced Meat Lettuce Wraps as a healthy alternative to heavier lunches. Packed with flavor and nutrients, they are perfect for a quick, delicious meal that won't weigh you down!

Spicy Chicken Wings with BBQ Sauce

Spice up your lunch with these Spicy Chicken Wings with BBQ Sauce. Perfectly crispy and coated with a smoky, spicy BBQ sauce, these wings offer a zesty kick to your midday meal. Quick and easy to prepare, they're a fantastic way to bring excitement to your dining table!

Servings: 1

Prepping Time: 10 minutes

Cook Time: 20 minutes

Difficulty: Easy

Ingredients:

- 6 chicken wings
- 1 tbsp olive oil
- 1 tsp chili powder
- 1/2 tsp garlic powder
- 1/2 tsp smoked paprika
- Salt and pepper to taste

- 1/4 cup BBQ sauce
- 1 tbsp honey

Step-by-Step Preparation:

1. Preheat your air fryer to 360°F (182°C).
2. Toss the chicken wings in a bowl with olive oil, chili powder, garlic powder, smoked paprika, salt, and pepper.
3. Place the wings in the air fryer basket and cook for 10 minutes. Flip the wings and cook for an additional 10 minutes until crispy.
4. In a small bowl, mix the BBQ sauce with honey.
5. Coat the cooked wings in the BBQ sauce mixture.
6. Return the wings to the air fryer for 2 more minutes to glaze.

Nutritional Facts: (Per serving)

- Calories: 480
- Protein: 24g
- Carbohydrates: 18g
- Fat: 34g
- Fiber: 1g
- Sugar: 15g

Enjoy these Spicy Chicken Wings with a side of your favorite crunchy vegetables or a light salad for a balanced, flavorful lunch. They're not just delicious; they're a mealtime adventure that's both satisfying and memorable!

Chapter 03: Air Fryer Dinner Recipes

Breaded German Wiener Schnitzel with Potatoes

Experience the authentic flavors of Germany with this Breaded German Wiener Schnitzel served with potatoes. This dish combines a crispy breaded veal cutlet with tender, seasoned potatoes for a hearty and satisfying dinner that's easy to prepare in your air fryer!

Servings: 1

Prepping Time: 15 minutes

Cook Time: 15 minutes

Difficulty: Easy

Ingredients:

- 1 veal cutlet, pounded thin
- 1/4 cup flour
- 1 egg, beaten

- 1/2 cup breadcrumbs
- 1/2 cup sliced potatoes
- 2 tbsp olive oil
- Salt and pepper to taste
- Lemon wedge for serving

Step-by-Step Preparation:

1. Season the veal cutlet with salt and pepper, then dredge in flour.
2. Dip the floured cutlet into the beaten egg, then coat with breadcrumbs.
3. Toss the sliced potatoes in 1 tbsp olive oil and season with salt and pepper.
4. Place the breaded cutlet and potatoes in the air fryer.
5. Cook at 400°F (204°C) for 15 minutes, flipping the schnitzel halfway through and shaking the potatoes occasionally, until the schnitzel is golden and crispy and the potatoes are tender.
6. Serve the schnitzel with a lemon wedge for squeezing over.

Nutritional Facts: (Per serving)

- Calories: 720
- Protein: 38g
- Carbohydrates: 58g
- Fat: 35g
- Fiber: 4g
- Sugar: 3g

Enjoy this Breaded German Wiener Schnitzel with a side of crispy potatoes for a dinner that brings a taste of Europe right to your table. This meal is perfect when you crave something traditional yet simple to prepare, ensuring a delightful dining experience every time!

Crispy Salt and Pepper Tofu

Indulge in the delicious simplicity of Crispy Salt and Pepper Tofu, enhanced with a kick of chili, scallions, and garlic. This dish combines subtle heat with savory flavors, making it a vibrant and satisfying dinner option that's quick and easy to prepare in your air fryer.

Servings: 1

Prepping Time: 10 minutes

Cook Time: 15 minutes

Difficulty: Easy

Ingredients:

- 1/2 block firm tofu, pressed and cubed
- 1 tbsp cornstarch
- 1/2 tsp salt
- 1/2 tsp cracked black pepper
- 1 small chili, finely sliced
- 2 scallions, chopped

- 2 cloves garlic, minced
- 1 tbsp vegetable oil
- 1 tsp sesame seeds (optional, for garnish)

Step-by-Step Preparation:

1. Toss the tofu cubes with cornstarch, salt, and pepper until evenly coated.
2. Preheat the air fryer to 380°F (193°C).
3. Spray or brush the air fryer basket with vegetable oil and add the tofu cubes.
4. Air fry for 15 minutes, shaking the basket halfway through, until the tofu is golden and crispy.
5. While the tofu cooks, heat the vegetable oil in a small pan over medium heat and sauté the garlic, chili, and scallions until fragrant and slightly softened.
6. Toss the crispy tofu with the sautéed chili, scallions, and garlic.
7. Garnish with sesame seeds if desired.

Nutritional Facts: (Per serving)

- Calories: 280
- Protein: 12g
- Carbohydrates: 18g
- Fat: 18g
- Fiber: 2g
- Sugar: 2g

This Crispy Salt and Pepper Tofu is a delightful dish combining crunchy texture and bold flavors. Whether you want a quick dinner or a delicious way to enjoy tofu, this recipe will surely impress. Enjoy it alone or as part of a larger meal for a truly satisfying experience!

Spaghetti Full Shrimp with Sundried Tomatoes

Treat yourself to a delightful fusion of flavors with Spaghetti Full Shrimp, complemented by the rich taste of sundried tomatoes and fresh spinach. This dish is an exquisite blend of seafood and pasta, perfect for a gourmet dinner that's surprisingly easy to whip up in your air fryer.

Servings: 1

Prepping Time: 10 minutes

Cook Time: 10 minutes

Difficulty: Easy

Ingredients:

- 1/2 cup cooked spaghetti
- 6 large shrimp, peeled and deveined
- 1/4 cup sundried tomatoes, chopped
- 1 cup fresh spinach
- 1 clove garlic, minced
- 1 tbsp olive oil

- Salt and pepper to taste
- 1 tbsp grated Parmesan cheese (optional)

Step-by-Step Preparation:

1. Toss the shrimp with olive oil, garlic, salt, and pepper.
2. Preheat the air fryer to 360°F (182°C).
3. Place the shrimp in the air fryer basket and cook for 5 minutes.
4. Add the sundried tomatoes and spinach to the basket with the shrimp and cook for 5 minutes until the shrimp are pink and fully cooked.
5. Toss the cooked spaghetti with the shrimp, sundried tomatoes, and spinach mixture.
6. Sprinkle with Parmesan cheese before serving, if desired.

Nutritional Facts: (Per serving)

- Calories: 420
- Protein: 25g
- Carbohydrates: 38g
- Fat: 20g
- Fiber: 4g
- Sugar: 5g

Savor this Spaghetti Full of Shrimp as a luxurious and satisfying meal that brings the essence of a fine dining experience to your home. Quick, delicious, and flavorful, it's an ideal choice for a special dinner or a nourishing treat!

Roasted Lamb Ribs with Spices and Greens

Savor the rich, deep flavors of Roasted Lamb Ribs with Spices and Greens, a dish that combines tender lamb with a robust spice blend and fresh greens. This recipe promises a hearty and refined dining experience, perfect for a dinner that impresses with minimal effort.

Servings: 1

Prepping Time: 15 minutes

Cook Time: 20 minutes

Difficulty: Easy

Ingredients:

- 4 lamb ribs
- 1 tbsp olive oil
- 1 tsp paprika
- 1/2 tsp garlic powder
- 1/2 tsp rosemary
- Salt and pepper to taste

- 1/2 cup mixed greens (like spinach and arugula)
- 1 tbsp balsamic vinegar

Step-by-Step Preparation:

1. Rub the lamb ribs with olive oil, paprika, garlic powder, rosemary, salt, and pepper.
2. Preheat the air fryer to 380°F (193°C).
3. Place the lamb ribs in the air fryer basket and cook for 20 minutes, flipping halfway through.
4. In the last 2 minutes of cooking, add the mixed greens to the air fryer to wilt slightly.
5. Drizzle the cooked greens with balsamic vinegar and serve alongside the lamb ribs.

Nutritional Facts: (Per serving)

- Calories: 610
- Protein: 24g
- Carbohydrates: 5g
- Fat: 55g
- Fiber: 1g
- Sugar: 2g

Enjoy these Roasted Lamb Ribs with a side of lightly seasoned greens for a fulfilling and flavorful meal. It's perfect for a cozy dinner, bringing the essence of gourmet cooking into the comfort of your kitchen!

Roasted Cornish Hen with Apples

Indulge in a delightful Roasted Cornish Hen with Apples, a dish that blends the succulent flavors of poultry with the sweet notes of apples for a truly enchanting dinner. This elegant yet simple recipe is perfect for those evenings when you want to treat yourself to something special.

Servings: 1

Prepping Time: 10 minutes

Cook Time: 25 minutes

Difficulty: Easy

Ingredients:

- 1 Cornish hen, halved
- 1 tbsp olive oil
- 1/2 tsp thyme
- Salt and pepper to taste
- 1 apple, sliced
- 1/2 onion, sliced

- 2 garlic cloves, minced

Step-by-Step Preparation:

1. Rub the Cornish hen with olive oil, thyme, salt, and pepper.
2. Preheat the air fryer to 360°F (182°C).
3. Arrange the Cornish hen in the air fryer basket, skin side up.
4. Scatter the apple, onion, and garlic around the hen.
5. Cook for 25 minutes or until the hen is golden and cooked through.
6. Halfway through cooking, gently stir the apples and onions to ensure even cooking.

Nutritional Facts: (Per serving)

- Calories: 510
- Protein: 38g
- Carbohydrates: 24g
- Fat: 30g
- Fiber: 3g
- Sugar: 16g

Enjoy this Roasted Cornish Hen with Apples for a luxurious dinner that combines the comforting flavors of roasted poultry with the natural sweetness of apples. This meal is a feast for the senses, perfect for a night or special occasion.

Roasted Pork with Potatoes

Relish the classic comfort of Roasted Pork with Potatoes, which epitomizes home-cooked goodness. Perfectly seasoned and roasted to perfection, this meal delivers tender pork paired with crispy golden potatoes, offering a hearty and satisfying dinner option.

Servings: 1

Prepping Time: 10 minutes

Cook Time: 25 minutes

Difficulty: Easy

Ingredients:

- 1 pork chop, about 1-inch thick
- 1/2 cup baby potatoes, halved
- 1 tbsp olive oil
- 1/2 tsp rosemary
- 1/2 tsp thyme
- Salt and pepper to taste

- 1 garlic clove, minced

Step-by-Step Preparation:

1. Rub the pork chop with half the olive oil, minced garlic, rosemary, thyme, salt, and pepper.
2. Toss the potatoes in olive oil and season with salt and pepper.
3. Preheat the air fryer to 380°F (193°C).
4. Place the pork chop in the air fryer and surround it with the seasoned potatoes.
5. Cook for 25 minutes, flipping the pork halfway through and stirring the potatoes occasionally until the pork is cooked and crispy.

Nutritional Facts: (Per serving)

- Calories: 540
- Protein: 35g
- Carbohydrates: 23g
- Fat: 34g
- Fiber: 2g
- Sugar: 1g

Savor this Roasted Pork with Potatoes as a delightful solo dinner. It brings traditional flavors and comforting warmth to your evening. It's a simple yet delicious meal perfect for relaxing after a long day.

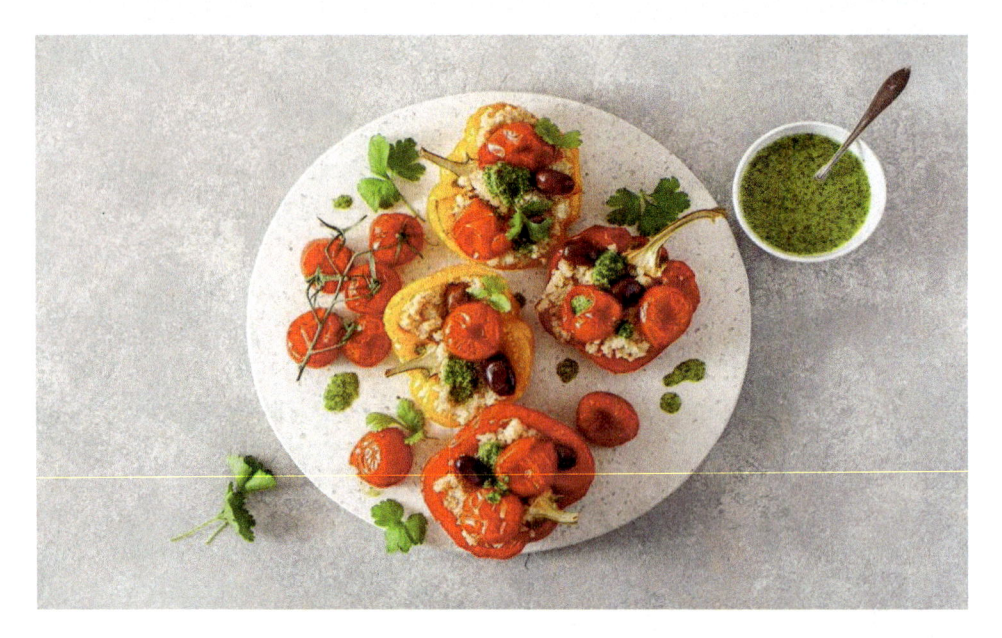

Stuffed Bell Peppers with Quinoa Tomatoes

Experience a burst of flavors with Stuffed Bell Peppers filled with a vibrant mix of quinoa, tomatoes, and olives and a zesty herb sauce chimichurri. This dish is colorful, delicious, and packed with nutrients, making it a perfect gourmet dinner for one.

Servings: 1

Prepping Time: 15 minutes

Cook Time: 15 minutes

Difficulty: Easy

Ingredients:

- 1 large bell pepper, top cut off and seeds removed
- 1/2 cup cooked quinoa
- 1/4 cup diced tomatoes
- 1/4 cup sliced black olives
- 2 tbsp chimichurri sauce
- 1 tbsp olive oil

- Salt and pepper to taste

Step-by-Step Preparation:

1. Mix the cooked quinoa, diced tomatoes, sliced olives, and 1 tbsp of chimichurri sauce in a bowl—season with salt and pepper.
2. Stuff the bell pepper with the quinoa mixture.
3. Drizzle olive oil over the stuffed pepper.
4. Preheat the air fryer to 360°F (182°C).
5. Place the stuffed bell pepper in the air fryer and cook for 15 minutes or until tender and the filling is heated.
6. Drizzle the remaining chimichurri sauce over the cooked stuffed pepper before serving.

Nutritional Facts: (Per serving)

- Calories: 280
- Protein: 6g
- Carbohydrates: 33g
- Fat: 15g
- Fiber: 6g
- Sugar: 6g

Enjoy this Stuffed Bell Pepper with Quinoa and a touch of chimichurri for a meal that is as nourishing as it is flavorful. This dish offers a beautiful blend of textures and tastes, perfect for a satisfying dinner that keeps you healthy and delighted.

Fried Cod Fillet with Asparagus and Tomatoes

Delight in the light and crisp Fried Cod Fillet served with tender asparagus and juicy tomatoes, epitomizing simplicity and flavor. This meal is a beautiful way to enjoy a wholesome dinner that's satisfying and nutritious, prepared effortlessly in your air fryer.

Servings: 1

Prepping Time: 10 minutes

Cook Time: 12 minutes

Difficulty: Easy

Ingredients:

- 1 cod fillet (about 6 ounces)
- 1/2 cup panko breadcrumbs
- 1 egg, beaten
- 1/2 cup asparagus, trimmed
- 1/2 cup cherry tomatoes
- 1 tbsp olive oil

- Salt and pepper to taste
- Lemon wedge for serving

Step-by-Step Preparation:

1. Season the cod fillet with salt and pepper.
2. Dip the fillet in the beaten egg, then coat with panko breadcrumbs.
3. Toss the asparagus and cherry tomatoes with olive oil and a pinch of salt.
4. Preheat the air fryer to 400°F (204°C).
5. Place the breaded cod and vegetable mixture in the air fryer basket.
6. Cook for 12 minutes until the cod is golden, flakes easily with a fork, and the vegetables are tender.
7. Serve immediately with a squeeze of lemon.

Nutritional Facts: (Per serving)

- Calories: 435
- Protein: 35g
- Carbohydrates: 32g
- Fat: 18g
- Fiber: 3g
- Sugar: 4g

Savor this Fried Cod Fillet with Asparagus and Tomatoes for a meal that combines freshness and convenience, perfect for a busy evening. This dish tastes terrific and supports a healthy lifestyle with lean protein and vibrant vegetables. Enjoy a gourmet dinner that feels effortless yet luxurious.

Beef and Broccoli Stir Fry

Experience the bold flavors of Beef and Broccoli Stir Fry, a classic Asian dish that brings the sizzle of tender beef and crisp broccoli to your dinner table. This quick and easy recipe transforms simple ingredients into a flavorful feast, perfect for a fulfilling solo meal.

Servings: 1

Prepping Time: 10 minutes

Cook Time: 10 minutes

Difficulty: Easy

Ingredients:

- 1/2 cup thinly sliced beef (such as flank steak or sirloin)
- 1 cup broccoli florets
- 1 tbsp soy sauce
- 1 tbsp oyster sauce
- 1 clove garlic, minced
- 1/2 tsp grated ginger

- 1 tsp sesame oil
- 1 tsp cornstarch
- 2 tbsp water
- Salt and pepper to taste

Step-by-Step Preparation:

1. Mix soy sauce, oyster sauce, garlic, ginger, sesame oil, cornstarch, and water in a small bowl to create the sauce.
2. Preheat the air fryer to 380°F (193°C).
3. Toss the beef slices and broccoli florets with the sauce. Ensure each piece is evenly coated.
4. Place the beef and broccoli in the air fryer basket.
5. Cook for 10 minutes, stirring halfway through, until the meat is cooked and the broccoli is tender-crisp.
6. Season with salt and pepper to taste before serving.

Nutritional Facts: (Per serving)

- Calories: 330
- Protein: 25g
- Carbohydrates: 15g
- Fat: 18g
- Fiber: 3g
- Sugar: 5g

Enjoy this Beef and Broccoli Stir Fry as a quick yet delicious dinner option without skipping on taste. Perfect for a busy evening, this dish brings together rich flavors and nutritious ingredients in a satisfying and easy-to-prepare meal.

Chicken and Bell Peppers in Skewers

Elevate your dinner with these colorful Chicken and Bell pepper skewers, a dish that perfectly marries simplicity with flavor. This meal features juicy chicken and crisp bell peppers, all grilled to perfection in your air fryer, making it a vibrant and healthy option for a quick and delicious dinner.

Servings: 1

Prepping Time: 15 minutes

Cook Time: 10 minutes

Difficulty: Easy

Ingredients:

- 1/2 cup chicken breast, cubed
- 1/2 red bell pepper, cubed
- 1/2 yellow bell pepper, cubed
- 1 tbsp olive oil
- 1 tsp paprika
- 1/2 tsp garlic powder

- Salt and pepper to taste
- Wooden skewers soaked in water for at least 30 minutes

Step-by-Step Preparation:

1. Preheat the air fryer to 400°F (204°C).
2. Mix the olive oil, paprika, garlic powder, salt, and pepper in a bowl.
3. Toss the chicken and bell pepper cubes in the seasoning mixture until well coated.
4. Thread the chicken and bell peppers alternately onto the skewers.
5. Place the skewers in the air fryer basket.
6. Cook for 10 minutes, turning halfway through, until the chicken is thoroughly cooked and the bell peppers are slightly charred.

Nutritional Facts: (Per serving)

- Calories: 265
- Protein: 23g
- Carbohydrates: 8g
- Fat: 16g
- Fiber: 2g
- Sugar: 4g

Relish these skewers' delightful combination of tender chicken and flavorful bell peppers. A perfect dish for a fuss-free yet satisfying dinner, it's sure to bring a splash of color and loads of flavor to your dining experience!

Chapter 04: Air Fryer Snacks Recipes

Fried Zucchini Sticks Chips

Dive into the crispy delight of Fried Zucchini Sticks, a snack that turns this humble vegetable into a crunchy, addictive treat. Perfect for a quick bite or a healthy alternative to traditional chips, these zucchini sticks are easy to make and satisfyingly delicious, especially when paired with your favorite dipping sauce.

Servings: 1

Prepping Time: 10 minutes

Cook Time: 8 minutes

Difficulty: Easy

Ingredients:

- 1 medium zucchini, cut into sticks
- 1/4 cup all-purpose flour
- 1 egg, beaten

- 1/2 cup breadcrumbs
- 1/2 tsp garlic powder
- Salt and pepper to taste
- Cooking spray

Step-by-Step Preparation:

1. Preheat the air fryer to 400°F (204°C).
2. Coat the zucchini sticks in flour, shaking off excess.
3. Dip them in the beaten egg, then dredge in breadcrumbs mixed with garlic powder, salt, and pepper.
4. Arrange the breaded zucchini sticks in a single layer in the air fryer basket. Spray lightly with cooking spray.
5. Air fry for 8 minutes, turning halfway through, until golden and crispy.
6. Serve hot, optionally, with a dipping sauce like marinara or ranch.

Nutritional Facts: (Per serving)

- Calories: 295
- Protein: 11g
- Carbohydrates: 42g
- Fat: 9g
- Fiber: 3g
- Sugar: 6g

Enjoy these Fried Zucchini Sticks as a fantastic snack with flavor and crunch. They're perfect for curbing your cravings in a healthier way and provide a delightful alternative to more calorie-dense snacks.

Sweet Potato Tater Tots with Ketchup

Indulge in the sweet and savory crunch of Sweet Potato Tater Tots, a delightful twist on a classic snack. These homemade tots, paired with the tangy zest of ketchup, provide a comforting bite perfect for any snacking occasion. Cooked in the air fryer, they offer a healthier alternative with all the crispy goodness.

Servings: 1

Prepping Time: 15 minutes

Cook Time: 15 minutes

Difficulty: Easy

Ingredients:

- 1 large sweet potato, peeled
- 1 tbsp olive oil
- 1/4 tsp paprika
- Salt and pepper to taste
- 2 tbsp cornstarch
- Ketchup for dipping

Step-by-Step Preparation:

1. Grate the sweet potato finely.
2. Mix the grated sweet potato with olive oil, paprika, salt, pepper, and cornstarch until well combined.
3. Form the mixture into tiny, bite-sized tots.
4. Preheat the air fryer to 400°F (204°C).
5. Arrange the tots in a single layer in the air fryer basket, ensuring they don't touch.
6. Cook for 15 minutes, shaking the basket halfway through to ensure even cooking.
7. Serve hot with ketchup on the side for dipping.

Nutritional Facts: (Per serving)

- Calories: 298
- Protein: 2g
- Carbohydrates: 45g
- Fat: 12g
- Fiber: 5g
- Sugar: 9g

Enjoy these Sweet Potato Tater Tots as a delicious snack or a fun side dish. Their crispy exterior and soft, sweet interior make them irresistible, especially when dipped in ketchup. Perfect for satisfying your cravings in a wholesome, delightful way!

Delicious Jalapeno Poppers

Ignite your taste buds with Delicious Jalapeño Poppers, a spicy and cheesy treat perfect for any snack. These poppers are stuffed with a creamy filling and wrapped in crispy bacon, delivering flavor with each bite. Cooked in the air fryer, they come out perfectly golden without the extra grease.

Servings: 1

Prepping Time: 15 minutes

Cook Time: 8 minutes

Difficulty: Easy

Ingredients:

- 3 jalapeños, halved and seeded
- 3 tbsp cream cheese
- 1/4 cup shredded cheddar cheese
- 3 slices bacon, halved
- 1/4 tsp garlic powder
- Salt and pepper to taste

Step-by-Step Preparation:

1. Mix cream cheese, cheddar cheese, garlic powder, salt, and pepper in a small bowl.
2. Fill each jalapeño half with the cheese mixture.
3. Wrap each stuffed jalapeño with a half slice of bacon, securing with a toothpick if necessary.
4. Preheat the air fryer to 390°F (199°C).
5. Place the poppers in the air fryer basket in a single layer.
6. Cook for 8 minutes or until the bacon is crispy and the peppers are tender.
7. Remove the poppers carefully, letting them cool slightly before serving.

Nutritional Facts: (Per serving)

- Calories: 345
- Protein: 15g
- Carbohydrates: 5g
- Fat: 30g
- Fiber: 1g
- Sugar: 2g

Savor these delicious Jalapeño Poppers as a fiery and indulgent snack. Whether you're enjoying a movie night or hosting a party, these poppers are sure to be a hit. They offer the perfect combination of heat and flavor that's both satisfying and irresistibly tasty!

Baked Mushrooms Stuffed

Savor the rich flavors of Baked Mushrooms Stuffed with chicken minced meat, cheese, and herbs. This delectable snack combines juicy mushrooms with savory fillings. This gourmet treat is perfect for a luxurious snack or a delightful appetizer. It can be easily prepared in your air fryer to achieve ideal tenderness and crispness.

Servings: 1

Prepping Time: 10 minutes

Cook Time: 10 minutes

Difficulty: Easy

Ingredients:

- 4 large mushrooms, stems removed
- 1/2 cup chicken minced meat
- 1/4 cup shredded cheese (your choice)
- 1 tbsp chopped fresh parsley
- 1 tbsp chopped fresh thyme

- 1 clove garlic, minced
- Salt and pepper to taste
- 1 tbsp olive oil

Step-by-Step Preparation:

1. Preheat the air fryer to 350°F (177°C).
2. Mix the minced chicken, shredded cheese, parsley, thyme, garlic, salt, and pepper in a bowl.
3. Stuff each mushroom cap generously with the chicken mixture.
4. Brush the outside of the mushrooms with olive oil.
5. Arrange the stuffed mushrooms in the air fryer basket.
6. Cook for 10 minutes or until the mushrooms are tender and the filling is cooked.
7. Serve warm.

Nutritional Facts: (Per serving)

- Calories: 325
- Protein: 22g
- Carbohydrates: 4g
- Fat: 25g
- Fiber: 1g
- Sugar: 2g

These Baked Mushrooms Stuffed with chicken minced meat, cheese, and herbs offer a deliciously sophisticated snack that's sure to impress. Enjoy the delightful blend of flavors and textures, perfect for an elegant snack or a special treat!

Coconut Shrimp with Dipping Sauces

Delight in the tropical taste of Coconut Shrimp, a crispy and sweet snack that brings the essence of the beach to your kitchen. Paired with various dipping sauces, these shrimps are a crunchy treat that's perfect for any occasion. Make them effortlessly in your air fryer for a healthier version of this beloved dish.

Servings: 1

Prepping Time: 15 minutes

Cook Time: 8 minutes

Difficulty: Easy

Ingredients:

- 6 large shrimp, peeled and deveined
- 1/4 cup all-purpose flour
- 1/2 tsp salt
- 1/4 tsp black pepper
- 1 egg, beaten
- 1/2 cup shredded coconut

- 1/2 cup panko breadcrumbs
- Cooking spray
- Dipping sauces (sweet chili sauce, mango salsa)

Step-by-Step Preparation:

1. Preheat the air fryer to 400°F (204°C).
2. Season the flour with salt and pepper.
3. Dredge each shrimp in the seasoned flour, dip it into the beaten egg, then coat it with a mixture of shredded coconut and panko breadcrumbs.
4. Spray the air fryer basket with cooking spray and place the shrimp in a single layer.
5. Cook for 8 minutes, flipping halfway through, until the shrimp are golden and crispy.
6. Serve hot with your choice of dipping sauces.

Nutritional Facts: (Per serving)

- Calories: 480
- Protein: 25g
- Carbohydrates: 53g
- Fat: 18g
- Fiber: 3g
- Sugar: 8g

Enjoy these delectable Coconut Shrimp as a festive and fun snack. Perfect for entertaining or a quick treat, they bring an irresistible burst of flavor and texture, especially when dipped into a sweet or tangy sauce!

Bacon Wrapped Dates with Goat Cheese

Indulge in the savory-sweet delight of Bacon Wrapped Dates stuffed with goat cheese. This tantalizing combination of creamy cheese, sweet dates, and crispy bacon makes a perfect bite-sized treat or appetizer, easily prepared in your air fryer for a touch of gourmet at any gathering.

Servings: 1

Prepping Time: 10 minutes

Cook Time: 10 minutes

Difficulty: Easy

Ingredients:

- 6 dates, pitted
- 3 slices of bacon, halved
- 3 tbsp goat cheese
- Toothpicks for securing

Step-by-Step Preparation:

1. Stuff each date with about 1/2 tablespoon of goat cheese.
2. Wrap each stuffed date with a half slice of bacon, securing it with a toothpick.
3. Preheat the air fryer to 375°F (190°C).
4. Place the bacon-wrapped dates in the air fryer basket in a single layer.
5. Cook for 10 minutes or until the bacon is crispy.
6. Serve immediately.

Nutritional Facts: (Per serving)

- Calories: 330
- Protein: 14g
- Carbohydrates: 27g
- Fat: 20g
- Fiber: 2g
- Sugar: 24g

Savor these Bacon-Wrapped Dates with Goat Cheese as an exquisite snack or appetizer. They perfectly balance the rich flavors of bacon and cheese with the natural sweetness of dates. They are sure to be a hit at any party or as a special treat just for you!

Buffalo Cauliflower Wings

Experience the bold and tangy flavor of Buffalo Cauliflower Wings, a vegetarian twist on a classic favorite. These bites are delicious and offer a healthier alternative to traditional wings. Perfectly crispy and drenched in spicy buffalo sauce, they're made effortlessly in your air fryer for a snack that satisfies without the guilt.

Servings: 1

Prepping Time: 10 minutes

Cook Time: 20 minutes

Difficulty: Easy

Ingredients:

- 1 cup cauliflower florets
- 1 tbsp olive oil
- 1/4 cup buffalo sauce
- 1 tsp garlic powder
- Salt and pepper to taste

- Ranch or blue cheese dressing for dipping
- Celery sticks for serving

Step-by-Step Preparation:

1. Toss the cauliflower florets with olive oil, garlic powder, salt, and pepper.
2. Preheat the air fryer to 360°F (182°C).
3. Arrange the cauliflower in the air fryer basket in a single layer.
4. Cook for 20 minutes, shaking the basket halfway through, until the cauliflower is crispy and golden.
5. Once cooked, toss the cauliflower in buffalo sauce until well coated.
6. Serve hot with ranch or blue cheese dressing and celery sticks on the side.

Nutritional Facts: (Per serving)

- Calories: 180
- Protein: 2g
- Carbohydrates: 10g
- Fat: 14g
- Fiber: 3g
- Sugar: 4g

Enjoy these Buffalo Cauliflower Wings as a spicy, flavorful snack that brings the heat without the meat. Perfect for game days, movie nights, or when you crave something deliciously different, these wings are a crowd-pleaser that everyone can enjoy!

Dried Apple Chips with Cinnamon

Delight in the sweet simplicity of Dried Apple Chips sprinkled with cinnamon, a wholesome and irresistible snack. These crisp, flavorful chips are a healthier alternative to processed snacks and capture the essence of fresh apples with a hint of spice. Made quickly in your air fryer, they are perfect for a nutritious nibble anytime.

Servings: 1

Prepping Time: 5 minutes

Cook Time: 15 minutes

Difficulty: Easy

Ingredients:

- 2 apples, thinly sliced
- 1/2 tsp ground cinnamon
- Cooking spray

Step-by-Step Preparation:

1. Lightly spray the air fryer basket with cooking spray.

2. Arrange the apple slices in a single layer in the basket.
3. Sprinkle the slices with ground cinnamon.
4. Set the air fryer to 300°F (150°C) and cook for 15 minutes, flipping the slices halfway through.
5. Continue cooking until the apple slices are dried and crispy.
6. Let them cool completely to crisp up further before serving.

Nutritional Facts: (Per serving)

- Calories: 95
- Protein: 0.5g
- Carbohydrates: 25g
- Fat: 0.3g
- Fiber: 4g
- Sugar: 18g

Enjoy these Dried Apple Chips with Cinnamon as a delightful, satisfying, and guilt-free treat. Perfect for curbing your sweet tooth or packing as a portable snack, these apple chips offer a delicious way to enjoy the natural sweetness of apples enhanced with a sprinkle of cinnamon.

Fried Crispy Onion Rings with Ketchup

Dive into the crunch of Fried Crispy Onion Rings, a classic snack always a crowd-pleaser. These golden rings are light and crunchy and perfectly paired with tangy ketchup for dipping. Using the air fryer, you get all the delightful crispiness with less oil, making it a more intelligent choice for snack time.

Servings: 1

Prepping Time: 10 minutes

Cook Time: 8 minutes

Difficulty: Easy

Ingredients:

- 1 large onion, cut into 1/4-inch rings
- 1/4 cup all-purpose flour
- 1 egg, beaten
- 1/2 cup breadcrumbs
- Salt to taste
- Cooking spray

- Ketchup for dipping

Step-by-Step Preparation:

1. Separate the onion slices into rings.
2. Dip each onion ring in flour, then the beaten egg, and finally coat with breadcrumbs.
3. Spray the air fryer basket with cooking spray.
4. Arrange the onion rings in a single layer in the basket.
5. Cook at 400°F (204°C) for 8 minutes, flipping halfway through.
6. Season with salt immediately after cooking.
7. Serve hot with ketchup on the side for dipping.

Nutritional Facts: (Per serving)

- Calories: 340
- Protein: 10g
- Carbohydrates: 53g
- Fat: 8g
- Fiber: 3g
- Sugar: 9g

Enjoy these Fried Crispy Onion Rings as a fantastic snack for a cozy night or when you need a tasty treat. They offer the perfect crunch and flavor, especially when dipped in your favorite ketchup!

Turkish Fried Borek Rolls with Meat Filling

Savor the rich and savory flavors of Turkish Fried Borek Rolls, filled with a delicious meat mixture. These crispy, golden rolls are a traditional Turkish delight, made more accessible and healthier in your air fryer. Perfect for a satisfying snack or a tempting appetizer, they will surely be a hit at any gathering or solo treat.

Servings: 1

Prepping Time: 20 minutes

Cook Time: 10 minutes

Difficulty: Easy

Ingredients:

- 3 sheets of filo pastry
- 1/2 cup ground beef
- 1 small onion, finely chopped
- 1 clove garlic, minced
- 1 tsp paprika

- 1/2 tsp cumin
- Salt and pepper to taste
- 2 tbsp olive oil
- Parsley for garnish (optional)

Step-by-Step Preparation:

1. Preheat the air fryer to 360°F (182°C).
2. In a skillet, heat 1 tbsp olive oil over medium heat. Add onion and garlic, and sauté until translucent.
3. Add ground beef, paprika, cumin, salt, and pepper. Cook until the meat is browned.
4. Cut filo sheets into strips about 3 inches wide. Place a spoonful of the meat mixture at one end of each strip.
5. Fold the filo over the filling to form triangles, continuing to fold like a flag until the strip is fully wrapped around the filling.
6. Brush the Borek rolls with the remaining olive oil.
7. Cook in the air fryer for 10 minutes, turning halfway through, until golden and crisp.
8. Garnish with parsley before serving, if desired.

Nutritional Facts: (Per serving)

- Calories: 580
- Protein: 24g
- Carbohydrates: 38g
- Fat: 36g
- Fiber: 2g
- Sugar: 2g

Enjoy these Turkish Fried Borek Rolls as a delightful snack infused with flavors and textures that transport you to the heart of Turkey. Perfect for satisfying your cravings with a touch of cultural flair!

Chapter 05: Air Fryer Appetizers Recipes

Grilled Violet Asparagus Wrapped with Bacon

Indulge in the elegance and simplicity of Grilled Violet Asparagus Wrapped with Bacon, a gourmet appetizer that combines the subtle sweetness of asparagus with the smoky richness of bacon. This dish cooks up quickly in your air fryer, perfect for impressing guests or treating yourself, offering a delightful blend of flavors and textures.

Servings: 1

Prepping Time: 5 minutes

Cook Time: 8 minutes

Difficulty: Easy

Ingredients:

- 6 violet asparagus spears, trimmed
- 3 slices of bacon, halved

- Salt and pepper to taste

Step-by-Step Preparation:

1. Wrap each asparagus spear with a half slice of bacon, securing it with a toothpick if necessary.
2. Season the wrapped asparagus lightly with salt and pepper.
3. Preheat the air fryer to 400°F (204°C).
4. Place the bacon-wrapped asparagus in the air fryer basket in a single layer.
5. Cook for 8 minutes, turning halfway through, until the bacon is crispy and the asparagus is tender.
6. Serve immediately.

Nutritional Facts: (Per serving)

- Calories: 180
- Protein: 12g
- Carbohydrates: 5g
- Fat: 12g
- Fiber: 2g
- Sugar: 2g

Enjoy this Grilled Violet Asparagus Wrapped with Bacon as a sophisticated appetizer that's visually appealing and delicious. Quick to prepare and packed with flavor, it's a sure way to elevate any meal or gathering.

Chicken Spinach Artichoke Creamy Soup

Warm up with a bowl of Chicken Spinach Artichoke Creamy Soup, a comforting and hearty dish that combines tender chicken, creamy artichokes, and nutritious spinach. This delicious soup is perfect for a cozy evening and can be easily made in your air fryer for a quick, one-pot meal that soothes and satisfies.

Servings: 1

Prepping Time: 10 minutes

Cook Time: 15 minutes

Difficulty: Easy

Ingredients:

- 1/2 cup cooked, shredded chicken
- 1/4 cup canned artichoke hearts, chopped
- 1/2 cup fresh spinach
- 1/2 cup chicken broth
- 1/4 cup heavy cream

- 1 clove garlic, minced
- 1 tbsp olive oil
- Salt and pepper to taste
- 1 tbsp grated Parmesan cheese (optional for topping)

Step-by-Step Preparation:

1. Preheat the air fryer to 350°F (177°C) using the bake setting.
2. Heat the olive oil in the air fryer's baking pan and sauté the minced garlic until fragrant.
3. Add the chicken broth, shredded chicken, and chopped artichoke hearts to the pan.
4. Cook for 10 minutes, stirring occasionally.
5. Stir in the spinach and heavy cream, cooking for 5 minutes until the spinach is wilted and the soup is heated.
6. Season with salt and pepper to taste.
7. Serve hot, sprinkled with grated Parmesan cheese if desired.

Nutritional Facts: (Per serving)

- Calories: 420
- Protein: 28g
- Carbohydrates: 9g
- Fat: 31g
- Fiber: 2g
- Sugar: 2g

Enjoy this Chicken Spinach Artichoke Creamy Soup as a luscious starter or a light meal. It's packed with flavor and wholesome ingredients, making it a nutritious choice that doesn't compromise taste. Perfect for a chilly day or a quick and satisfying comfort food fix!

Seafood Mini Crab Cake Balls

Dive into the delightful taste of the ocean with Seafood Mini Crab Cake Balls accompanied by a creamy tartar sauce. These bite-sized treats are perfect for seafood lovers, offering a crispy exterior and a succulent crab filling. Easily prepared in your air fryer, they make a chic and tasty appetizer for any occasion.

Servings: 1

Prepping Time: 15 minutes

Cook Time: 10 minutes

Difficulty: Easy

Ingredients:

- 1/2 cup crabmeat, drained and flaked
- 1/4 cup breadcrumbs
- 1 egg, beaten
- 1 tbsp mayonnaise
- 1 tsp Dijon mustard

- 1 tsp lemon juice
- 1/2 tsp Old Bay seasoning
- Salt and pepper to taste
- 2 tbsp tartar sauce for dipping

Step-by-Step Preparation:

1. Combine crabmeat, breadcrumbs, egg, mayonnaise, Dijon mustard, lemon juice, Old Bay seasoning, salt, and pepper in a bowl.
2. Mix thoroughly until the ingredients are well blended.
3. Form the mixture into small, bite-sized balls.
4. Preheat the air fryer to 400°F (204°C).
5. Place the crab cake balls in the air fryer basket, ensuring they do not touch.
6. Cook for 10 minutes, flipping halfway through, until golden and crispy.
7. Serve hot with tartar sauce for dipping.

Nutritional Facts: (Per serving)

- Calories: 330
- Protein: 20g
- Carbohydrates: 24g
- Fat: 16g
- Fiber: 1g
- Sugar: 2g

Enjoy these Seafood Mini Crab Cake Balls as a sophisticated and flavorful starter or a fun party snack. Their crispy texture and rich taste are sure to impress, making them a perfect choice for an elegant treat.

Barbecue Chicken Flatbreads with Red Onion

Savor the irresistible flavors in this Barbecue Chicken Flatbread, topped with tangy red onion and fresh cilantro. This dish brings together the sweetness of barbecue sauce with tender chicken and a crisp flatbread base, creating a perfect snack or light meal that's quick and easy to prepare in your air fryer.

Servings: 1

Prepping Time: 10 minutes

Cook Time: 8 minutes

Difficulty: Easy

Ingredients:

- 1 small flatbread
- 1/4 cup cooked, shredded chicken
- 2 tbsp barbecue sauce
- 1/4 red onion, thinly sliced
- 1/4 cup shredded mozzarella cheese
- 1 tbsp chopped cilantro

- Salt and pepper to taste

Step-by-Step Preparation:

1. Spread the barbecue sauce evenly over the flatbread.
2. Top with shredded chicken and sliced red onion.
3. Sprinkle mozzarella cheese over the top.
4. Season with salt and pepper.
5. Preheat the air fryer to 360°F (182°C).
6. Place the flatbread in the air fryer basket and cook for 8 minutes until the cheese is melted and the edges are crispy.
7. Garnish with chopped cilantro before serving.

Nutritional Facts: (Per serving)

- Calories: 385
- Protein: 22g
- Carbohydrates: 44g
- Fat: 14g
- Fiber: 2g
- Sugar: 12g

Enjoy this Barbecue Chicken Flatbread as a delightful snack or a quick dinner option. Its smoky barbecue flavor, cilantro's freshness, and red onion's sharpness make it a sure favorite for any occasion. It provides a satisfying and flavorful experience.

Spicy Korean Chicken Drumsticks

Ignite your taste buds with Spicy Korean Chicken Drumsticks, a fiery and flavorful dish that marries the zest of Korean spices with the juiciness of chicken. Perfectly cooked in your air fryer, these drumsticks offer a crispy exterior and a tender, moist interior, making them an irresistible appetizer or a satisfying meal.

Servings: 1

Prepping Time: 15 minutes (plus marinating time)

Cook Time: 20 minutes

Difficulty: Easy

Ingredients:

- 2 chicken drumsticks
- 2 tbsp Korean gochujang (red chili paste)
- 1 tbsp soy sauce
- 1 tbsp honey
- 1 clove garlic, minced

- 1 tsp sesame oil
- 1/2 tsp grated ginger
- Sesame seeds for garnish
- Sliced green onions for garnish

Step-by-Step Preparation:

1. Mix gochujang, soy sauce, honey, garlic, sesame oil, and ginger in a bowl to create the marinade.
2. Coat the drumsticks in the marinade and let them sit in the refrigerator for at least 30 minutes.
3. Preheat the air fryer to 380°F (193°C).
4. Place the marinated drumsticks in the air fryer basket.
5. Cook for 20 minutes, turning halfway through, until the drumsticks are cooked through and the outside is crispy.
6. Garnish with sesame seeds and green onions before serving.

Nutritional Facts: (Per serving)

- Calories: 310
- Protein: 28g
- Carbohydrates: 15g
- Fat: 15g
- Fiber: 1g
- Sugar: 10g

Enjoy these Spicy Korean Chicken Drumsticks as a bold and delicious treat. Whether you're looking for a vibrant starter or a main dish with a kick, these drumsticks are sure to satisfy your cravings with their intense flavors and perfect texture.

Chicken Mushroom Stuffed Peppers

Enjoy a delightful harmony of flavors with Chicken Mushroom Stuffed Peppers, a wholesome and delicious dish. This recipe features bell peppers filled to the brim with a savory mixture of chicken, mushrooms, and spices, all cooked to perfection in your air fryer. It's a colorful and nutritious option for a satisfying appetizer or a light meal.

> **Servings:** 1
>
> **Prepping Time:** 15 minutes
>
> **Cook Time:** 15 minutes
>
> **Difficulty:** Easy

Ingredients:

- 1 large bell pepper, halved and seeded
- 1/2 cup cooked, finely chopped chicken breast
- 1/4 cup chopped mushrooms
- 1 tbsp chopped onion
- 1 clove garlic, minced

- 1/4 cup shredded mozzarella cheese
- 1 tbsp olive oil
- Salt and pepper to taste
- 1 tbsp fresh parsley, chopped (for garnish)

Step-by-Step Preparation:

1. Preheat the air fryer to 360°F (182°C).
2. In a skillet, heat olive oil over medium heat. Sauté onion, garlic, and mushrooms until softened.
3. Mix the chicken, salt, and pepper, and cook for another 2 minutes.
4. Stuff the halved bell peppers with the chicken and mushroom mixture.
5. Top each half with shredded mozzarella cheese.
6. Place the stuffed peppers in the air fryer basket.
7. Cook for 15 minutes or until the peppers are tender and the cheese is melted and bubbly.
8. Garnish with chopped parsley before serving.

Nutritional Facts: (Per serving)

- Calories: 385
- Protein: 28g
- Carbohydrates: 15g
- Fat: 24g
- Fiber: 3g
- Sugar: 7g

Relish these Chicken Mushroom Stuffed Peppers as a flavorful and hearty dish that's easy to make and pleasing to the palate. These stuffed peppers are sure to delight with their robust flavors and vibrant presentation, perfect for a cozy night in or as a nutritious addition to your meal.

Mozzarella Breaded Sticks

Bite into the crispy, cheesy delight of Mozzarella Breaded Sticks, perfectly golden brown and delicious. Made in your air fryer, these sticks are a crowd-pleaser that combines the gooey richness of mozzarella with a crisp breadcrumb coating. Ideal for a snack or party appetizer, they're quick to prepare and sure to disappear just as fast!

Servings: 1

Prepping Time: 10 minutes

Cook Time: 6 minutes

Difficulty: Easy

Ingredients:

- 4 mozzarella sticks
- 1/4 cup all-purpose flour
- 1 egg, beaten
- 1/2 cup breadcrumbs
- 1/2 tsp Italian seasoning

- Salt to taste
- Cooking spray

Step-by-Step Preparation:

1. Freeze the mozzarella sticks for about an hour.
2. Dip each frozen mozzarella stick in flour, then into the beaten egg, and finally, thoroughly coat with breadcrumbs mixed with Italian seasoning and salt.
3. Spray the air fryer basket with cooking spray to prevent sticking.
4. Place the breaded mozzarella sticks in the air fryer basket.
5. Cook at 390°F (199°C) for 6 minutes or until golden brown and crispy.
6. Serve immediately with marinara sauce or your favorite dipping sauce.

Nutritional Facts: (Per serving)

- Calories: 420
- Protein: 28g
- Carbohydrates: 34g
- Fat: 18g
- Fiber: 2g
- Sugar: 4g

Enjoy these Mozzarella-Breaded Sticks as a golden, crispy treat perfect for any occasion. Whether you're hosting a gathering or just indulging yourself, these cheese sticks offer a delicious blend of comfort and flavor that's both satisfying and irresistibly tasty.

Crispy Garlic Bacon Bread

Savor the irresistible flavors of Crispy Garlic Bacon Bread, a heavenly combination of garlic's aroma and the savory crunch of bacon. This appetizer turns ordinary bread into an extraordinary treat, easily crafted in your air fryer for a crispy finish perfect for any snack time or gathering.

Servings: 1

Prepping Time: 5 minutes

Cook Time: 8 minutes

Difficulty: Easy

Ingredients:

- 2 slices of thick-cut bread
- 2 slices of bacon, finely chopped
- 1 clove garlic, minced
- 1 tbsp butter, softened
- 1 tbsp grated Parmesan cheese
- Parsley, chopped (for garnish)

Step-by-Step Preparation:

1. Preheat the air fryer to 350°F (177°C).
2. In a small pan, cook the chopped bacon until crispy. Remove and drain on paper towels.
3. Mix the softened butter with minced garlic and spread evenly over each slice of bread.
4. Top the buttered bread with cooked bacon and sprinkle with Parmesan cheese.
5. Place the prepared bread slices in the air fryer basket.
6. Cook for 8 minutes or until the bread is golden brown and crispy.
7. Garnish with chopped parsley before serving.

Nutritional Facts: (Per serving)

- Calories: 320
- Protein: 15g
- Carbohydrates: 30g
- Fat: 16g
- Fiber: 2g
- Sugar: 3g

Indulge in this Crispy Garlic Bacon Bread as a delightful appetizer or a luxurious snack. Its combination of crunchy textures and robust flavors makes it a crowd-pleaser that's both easy to prepare and deliciously satisfying. Perfect for an evening treat or as a side to your favorite meal!

Roasted Fig Halves with Drizzle Honey

Delve into the sweet, succulent world of Roasted Fig Halves with Honey Drizzle, a luxurious treat that combines the natural sweetness of figs with the rich flavor of honey. This dish is simple yet incredibly decadent, prepared quickly in your air fryer for a delightful appetizer or a sweet end to any meal.

Servings: 1

Prepping Time: 5 minutes

Cook Time: 6 minutes

Difficulty: Easy

Ingredients:

- 4 fresh figs, halved
- 2 tbsp honey
- 1 tbsp crushed walnuts (optional)
- A pinch of cinnamon

Step-by-Step Preparation:

1. Preheat the air fryer to 360°F (182°C).
2. Place the fig halves cut-side up in the air fryer basket.
3. Cook for 6 minutes or until the figs are soft and slightly caramelized.
4. Drizzle honey over the warm fig halves.
5. Sprinkle with cinnamon and crushed walnuts if using.

Nutritional Facts: (Per serving)

- Calories: 270
- Protein: 1g
- Carbohydrates: 68g
- Fat: 1g
- Fiber: 5g
- Sugar: 62g

Enjoy these Roasted Fig Halves with Honey Drizzle as an elegant snack or a refined appetizer. Their warm, gooey sweetness, enhanced by the subtle spice of cinnamon and the crunch of walnuts, makes them an exceptional treat for any occasion.

Stir-fried Beef with Vegetables

Explore the vibrant flavors of Stir-Fried Beef with Vegetables, a dynamic dish that combines tender beef with crisp, colorful veggies. This quick and nutritious appetizer is perfect for a healthy bite, combining protein-rich meat with a medley of vegetables cooked perfectly in your air fryer.

Servings: 1

Prepping Time: 10 minutes

Cook Time: 8 minutes

Difficulty: Easy

Ingredients:

- 1/2 cup thinly sliced beef (such as flank or sirloin)
- 1/4 cup sliced bell peppers
- 1/4 cup broccoli florets
- 1/4 cup sliced carrots
- 1 tbsp soy sauce
- 1 tsp sesame oil

- 1 garlic clove, minced
- 1 tsp ginger, grated
- Salt and pepper to taste

Step-by-Step Preparation:

1. Mix the marinade in a small bowl of soy sauce, sesame oil, garlic, and ginger.
2. Toss the beef slices in the marinade and sit for at least 5 minutes.
3. Preheat the air fryer to 400°F (204°C).
4. Place the marinated beef and all vegetables in the air fryer basket.
5. Cook for 8 minutes, shaking the basket halfway through to ensure even cooking.
6. Season with salt and pepper to taste before serving.

Nutritional Facts: (Per serving)

- Calories: 235
- Protein: 23g
- Carbohydrates: 10g
- Fat: 12g
- Fiber: 2g
- Sugar: 5g

Enjoy this Stir-Fried Beef with Vegetables as a fulfilling appetizer or a light main course. It's a quick, easy, and satisfying way to enjoy a well-rounded meal with flavor and good health. Perfect for a busy day or a speedy, delicious meal.

Conclusion

As we conclude this culinary journey through the "Solo Air Fryer Cookbook: Perfectly Portioned Recipes for One," I hope you've discovered the joy and simplicity of single-serving cooking with your air fryer. Each recipe was crafted with care to ensure that you can enjoy a variety of flavors and textures, all tailored to fit a solo lifestyle without sacrificing taste or nutrition.

From sizzling breakfasts that kickstart your morning to sumptuous dinners that wrap up your day with satisfaction and not forgetting the sweet treats that can brighten any moment, this cookbook is designed to make every meal an opportunity to treat yourself to delicious, well-portioned dishes. The power and versatility of the air fryer have transformed these recipes into quick, easy, and healthy alternatives to traditional cooking methods, helping you save time while reducing calorie intake.

Remember, cooking for one doesn't mean cutting corners on health or flavor. The recipes in this book leverage the air fryer's ability to cook with less oil, meaning each dish tastes great and contributes to a healthier lifestyle. Whether you are a beginner or an experienced cook, straightforward instructions and helpful tips have made your time in the kitchen enjoyable and effective.

Thank you for choosing this book as your guide to solo air frying. Continue to explore the diverse recipes, experiment with flavors, and, most importantly, enjoy every bite of your creations. Your air fryer is a gateway to culinary creativity, and with "Quick & Easy, Single-Serve Meals with Original Images," you're well-equipped to face any meal with enthusiasm and confidence.

Printed in Great Britain
by Amazon